AF698415

Tears for the Fallen 1914 - 1918

STEVEN LESLIE HILL

An environmentally friendly book printed and bound in England by
www.printondemand-worldwide.com

Mixed Sources
Product group from well-managed forests, and other controlled sources
www.fsc.org Cert no. TT-COC-002641
© 1996 Forest Stewardship Council
FSC

PEFC Certified
This product is from sustainably managed forests and controlled sources
www.pefc.org
PEFC

This book is made entirely of chain-of-custody materials

FastPrint Publishing
www.fast-print.net/store.php

Tears for the Fallen 1914 - 1918

Copyright © Steven Leslie Hill 2012

All rights reserved

No part of this book may be reproduced in any form by photocopying or any electronic or mechanical means, including information storage or retrieval systems, without permission in writing from both the copyright owner and the publisher of the book.

ISBN 978-178035-471-2

First published 2012 by
FASTPRINT PUBLISHING
Peterborough, England.

This book is dedicated to
All the Fallen
Of
1914 – 1918

Introduction

The war of 1914-1918 was an unprecedented slaughter of human life. The troops mobilised from both sides for this carnage was in the region of 65 million of which at least half of that number would become wounded, missing or dead.

Since the dawn of time, mankind has been in conflict and war. From the early 'slings and arrows' to the present day threat of terrorism and nuclear annihilation, war has been, and still is, a constant shadow in the lives of the human race. Until 1914, and the outbreak of World War One, most battles and conflicts were fought by invading armies which would meet on designated ground with the winner taking the 'spoils' as conqueror.

From the Romans, through to the Napoleonic period, although many countries would be on opposite sides, no war could be truly called a World War. However, in 1914, all that was to change as nations from across the globe complete with new, more devastating weaponry in the form of aircraft, ships, tanks, submarines, machine guns and the introduction of chemical weapons in the shape of phosgene, chlorine and mustard gas joined their respective side to fight the first total World War.

The legacy of that conflict, followed by the Second World War which terrifyingly introduced the human race to the nuclear age, is still with us as nations still develop and threaten the use of weapons of mass destruction. This, combined with international terrorism, makes the present and future world a very unstable and insecure place to inhabit.

The following poems I have written are a condemnation of the madness of World War One and indeed all subsequent wars that have followed and the suffering that they bring. They are also a tribute to the individuals of the Great War of 1914-1918, who fought with great courage, bravery and compassion for a peaceful, tolerant and free world.

Lest we forget

S.L.H.

Acknowledgements

I would like to express my sincere gratitude to the following people whose contribution has made this book possible.

Tim Priestley – Chairman Chesterfield Branch Western Front Association
Cover photograph and initial proof reading.

Geoff & Miriam Street – School Head Teachers (Retired)
For their final proof reading of my work.

Fast Print Publishing
For their excellent service and finished product.

Susan Hill (My English Rose)
For her initial layout work, typing, love and support throughout.

Tears For The Fallen

British Soldier

The cannons no longer roar
Fighting now all gone
I stand here in 'no man's land'
And look at this hell called The Somme

For three years now
I have survived this place
And the lines of an old man
Now scar my young face

I think of comrades fallen
And the tears begin to swell
Of the laughter and the young lives
Of friends I knew so well

'Old Pals', we were together
And on each other we did depend
But I am the only one left standing here
At this war's end

So I will cry my tears for the fallen
And wish their souls peace on high
And hope one day we will meet again
When it's my turn to die

Poppies

Where they have fallen
We will grow
On this scared battlefield
Where the four seasons blow

Our stems stand tall
To the memory of the dead
Our petals the colour
Of the blood that they shed

So if their mortal remains
Are never found or given a final grave
Then forever we will mark the place
Of the passing of the brave

A Call To Arms

1914
British Infantry

We march in a column
Down the main street of the town
Thousands of cheering people
Fill the air with a patriotic, happy sound

Young girls throwing flowers
A kiss for some soldiers too
Small children skipping beside us
What little they all knew

For a place called hell awaits us
In the sodden mud of Flanders fields
A place of death and destruction
Where young lives war robs and steals

And as we walk along
Past the crowd and the town hall band
I wonder how many marching here
Will return to this green and pleasant land?

But for now I will enjoy the moment
And a feeling of national pride
As we comrades walk together
Into history, side by side.

Goodbye Sweet Love

I lie back here in this trench
And look at the sky so blue
And as my life passes before me
My thoughts turn to you

Your hair of gold like summer corn
With eyes of turquoise blue
The gentle touch of your hand
And lips sweet as morning dew

What I would have given, my love
To have seen you just one more time
But sadly as I lie here
Mortal life will soon be no longer mine

For the angels are now taking me
To a staircase of golden light
And a tranquil peace now surrounds me
And I have lost my will to fight

So goodbye my sweet love
Goodbye forever more
Please feel the final kiss from my soul
As I walk through Heaven's door

The Grim Reaper

Australian Soldier

The very first time I saw him
He took my friend's dying hand
On the beach at Gallipoli
Amongst the carnage on the sand

Then he appeared again month's later
Out in 'no man's land' on The Somme
As he scythed down more good men's lives
And took their souls away, one by one

At Broodseinde, Bellicourt and Ypres
Again, I watched his work
As more young soldiers joined his ranks
When they fell in the mud and dirt

Now alone in the darkness
I see he's here and looking for me
And there is nowhere to run to,
Hide or be free

So if my soul is to be taken
And into that dark void finally hurled
Then make sure that future generations remember
Every time Australia's flag is unfurled

Dedicated to the Australian Infantry who fought with great courage and distinction in some of the bloodiest battles of the Great War

Burial Party

German Officer
Verdun

The trench is dug
And we prepare their grave
Our men line up
To pay respects to the brave

For although they were our enemy
They fought to the last
Now their lives are gone
A thing of the past

So we salute their courage
And the sacrifice they made
For the glory of France
Their lives they gave

And we say a few words
To the God we all share
And send forth their souls
To his divine heavenly care

Then it's all over
Back to as before
To the maiming and the killing
Of this so called 'Great War'

Inspired and dedicated to the French Infantry Unit at Verdun, who were buried as a mark of respect by their German opposition and whose grave is now a public monument known as the 'Trench of Bayonets'.

Also, to the 6 million French Soldiers who were casualties of the Great War.

French Tenor

German Infantry

A warm summer evening
Out here on The Somme
The day's machine gun and cannon fire
Had at last quietened down and done

Then in the quietness across "no man's land"
Only a short distance from our line
Came the most beautiful voice of a Frenchman
Singing about a happier time

We all watched and listened
To this wonderful tenor voice
For just like us these French boys
Are not here out of choice

And when he had finished his song
All about peace and love
You could at least for a small while
Believe in a God above

"Merci" he called across to us
As we applauded and asked for more
For we all know that tomorrow at dawn
It will be both sides back to war

Inspired by an Officer of the German Army

Lice

Lice, bloody lice
Bloody lice everywhere
Our bodies covered in these parasites
Over our flesh and in our hair

Itching and scratching
Until our skin it bleeds with sores
As these disgusting creatures
Gorge their fill on what is yours

I would rather face the trench rats
Than have this filth on my bones
As they move from soldier to soldier
Looking for new homes

If there is any consolation
It's that the Germans are just the same
Lousy and filthy just like us
And knee deep in mud and rain

Bloody War

Images of war
Flash through my head
As I lie in this ward's
Hospital bed

Sounds of cannon fire
And machine gun too
Mixed with screams
Of friends that I knew

It's like my own newsreel
Inside my head
Showing me the twisted bodies
Of the wounded and dead

They said it would be over by Christmas
How little they knew
Just how difficult a war it would be
And what we would go through

Just seventeen
I volunteered to fight
And how I regret that day now
When I turn out the light

Knee deep in water, mud and ice
My body covered in parasites and lice
Rats in battalions feed on the dead
'Your Country Needs You'
Lord Kitchener said

Horror and carnage
I can't take any more
Will I ever leave
This 'bloody war'?

Dedicated to the millions of solders who suffered from shell shock (P.T.S.D) and spent the remainder of their lives in mental torment following their experiences on the front line.

Angel Of Albert

Standing here as the rain
Soaks the ground
I look at what remains
Of this once vibrant town

Now reduced to rubble
A twisted and blackened shell
It looks like a dwelling place
Reserved for those in hell

But like some holy miracle
The Virgin's statue she looks down
From her place high upon
The Basilica of this town

No shell or shot can touch her
As she leans over from her place
And there seems almost a look of sorrow
And tears on her face

For amongst this death and destruction
She seems protected by God's hand
Gently weeping for this scorched
And battered land

And when this war is over
People will talk of her down the years
The Holy Angel of Albert
With her eyes full of tears

This small town was the gateway to the Somme for allied troops and its famous statue of the Virgin and Child was filled with superstition that should it fall, the war would end. The town changed hands from British to German and then back to British, and the statue fell in April 1918, several months before Armistice Day.

War's Bitter Harvest

Like the fruit on a tree
Young men like you and me
Are picked when ripe
And still bursting with life

Like the corn in a field
To the beast of war our lives we yield
And are cut down
When ripe and still bursting with life

Like the fish in the sea
We are caught, young and free
And are killed when fresh
And still bursting with life

But like an old decaying tree
Our lives will never be
For we were taken when young
And still bursting with life

Known Only To God

Passchendaele

I want to see the summer sun of England
In a cloudless blue sky
To walk the green fields of my country
Just once more, before I die

To stand on its beaches
See the sea as it crashes the shore
A stone castle on the headland
To feel it all once more

The beauty of the Dales
Its lakes, moorland and heath
Chalk white cliffs of Dover
And hear church bells tolling for peace

Oak trees that reach the skyline
Woods of Alder, Beech and Yew
Springtime carpet of flowers
And the scent of fresh morning dew

But, alas, I will never see any
For my body is scattered somewhere in the mud
And on my headstone it reads
'Known only to God above'

Dedicated to the thousands of British and Commonwealth Soldiers
Who died in the 'hell' of Passchendaele

French Village

French Infantry

Wet mist shrouds the cold, hard night
Derelict stone church and houses awash in clear moonlight
Mud covered roads and fire charred stumps of trees
The sound of distant cannon fire carries on the breeze

From our position
Which we have held now for several days
I look at this once proud village
Now a wasted ruin, bathed in misty haze

It would once have been the home
Of so many happy souls
Now it's just a bomb site
Full of rubble and shell holes

A place of peace and laughter
Of children, work and play
Turned into a battleground
Where good men die each day

So for our nation's future
We will take revenge at every chance
And fight for our country's liberty
And for the honour of France

Gas Attack

British Infantry 1915

Dawns light on The Somme
The morning clear and bright
Our officer gave the order
"Stand to and prepare to fight!"

Then the German guns began to thunder
And the shells began to burst
Soon the boys in our line
Were gripped by a terrible thirst

We received the order
Go to the front line straight away
And I will never forget
What I saw that terrible day

Men blind and screaming
Foaming from mouth, nose and ear
Dying a grotesque and painful death
Their faces full of fear

We worked quickly
To remove the wounded away
Amidst a hail of artillery shells
It took us most of the day

And I will forever remember those boys
And the price they had to pay
For their images are still in my mind
And it seems they are here to stay

Fields

Out in the fields
Where the red poppies grow
Now no longer covered
In mud, rain and snow

No more destruction
Shell holes and wire
No more young lives
Consumed in the fire

Now the only sound
Is of bird song and bees
And the gentle leaf rustle
Of summer's green trees

For in these fields
Lie the brave and the best
A place where the fallen
Forever will rest

Gallipoli

Anzac Infantry
1915

It was said this campaign
Would change the war
But alas it was not to be
And thousands of men
Gave up their lives
On the beaches at Gallipoli

The Turks held the high ground
And defended it good and well
The troops landed on the beach
To a cannon and machine gun hell

The campaign was a blunder
On a monumental scale
That cost the lives of many men
And from the beginning doomed to fail

After months of intense fighting
The order was given to withdraw
And under constant cannon shell
They returned to ships offshore

Known as the 'Bloody Dardanelles'
And now part of history
It will be remembered always
For the slaughter at Gallipoli

Dedicated to the memory of all the New Zealand and Australian Troops who lost their lives during the campaign

Love Letter

From The Somme

My Darling Hannah,

I write this short letter tonight, for tomorrow at dawn we go over the top to fight.

I want you to know that you are my love to hold, a beauty with a soul and a heart of gold. A gentleness of touch and an angel's kiss. The day I met you, I knew I had been granted my perfect wish.

So feel my love, and if I should die, know it will never grow old as the years go by, but will burn like a beacon, a torch in the dark, and know I will always love you straight from the heart.

Yours, with love
John

The Good Book

United States' Soldier

I came across this German
Lying dead in 'no man's land'
And he had a Holy Bible
Wide open in his hand

His eyes they stared vacant
And lifeless at the sky
And I thought how comforting it must have been
To recite a prayer before you die

So I closed his eyes gently
And took the 'good book' from his hands
And made my way back to our lines
Across this blood soaked land

I never knew who he was
Or where he had come from
All I know he was a man, just like me
But for him this war is done

A Man I Know Well

This is a short verse
About a man I know well
Who always had a ready smile
And a good story he could always tell

A heart strong and full of life
That beat with the passion of youth
A man who walked tall and proud
Always sought justice, freedom and truth

But now his life is over
A simple statistic of this war
Whose widow will receive his medal
In a ceremony at the local town hall

But in truth, he died for nothing
In a war of politics and greed
Whose wife is now left alone
With three younger mouths to feed

For I am the man of this verse
And on the battlefield somewhere I lay
Never to walk again with my love
Or see the sun rise each day

So I say a last farewell
As from this life my soul is set free
And go on my final journey
Away from war and all its misery

Lost Generation

British Soldier

My Lewis Gun opens up
Backed by artillery fire
And their bodies start to
Pile up, entangled in our wire

Like us these poor souls
Give up their lives
In this ritual slaughter
On both sides

To describe such madness
Mere words cannot say
As this young generation
By the thousands are murdered each day

Sadly these young boys
Will soon be young no more
A wasted generation
What the hell is it all for?

English Spring Dawn

Dawn rises
Above the village green
The barn owl finishes the 'night shift'
And disappears unseen

In the fields the lapwing's call
And hares, they shadow box
Rabbits, pheasants, partridge
And one sly, old fox

Bats return to the belfry
As a kingfisher works the stream
Warm spring sunshine
Over a landscape so green

Butterflies and bees
And budding new trees
The skylark sings out
From a perfect blue sky

But as the darkness fades away
And the new day begins
The Officer's sharp whistle suddenly wakens me
From my distant thoughts and dreams

So out of our trench we go
To fight this wretched war
My English spring dawn I hope and pray
I will live to see once more

Trenches Of Death

British Infantry

Above our trench a flare lights up the night
The familiar features of 'no man's land'
Glow for a moment
Clear and bright

For tomorrow at 6 a.m.
We will go over the top
And many a good man here tonight
A bullet he will stop

What's it all for
This damned war?
Killing each other it seems
For little or nothing at all

So if tomorrow I am to die
Then like that flare
Let my soul
Brighten the sky

For when it's all over
And all the killing's done
Dear God take our spirits
To that peaceful place
Where forever we can rest in the sun

Sniper

I have been here now
For well over an hour
Lying concealed just in front
Of their barbed wire

Holding my rifle
I slowly scope their line
It's all about patience
Just a matter of time

Then I see movement
And my target is clear
He stands there smiling
He shows no fear

I watch him talking
To his comrades and friends
But I am about to make
His young life end

I don't really hate him
Or care where he's from
He is simply the enemy
And I hold the gun

So I release the trigger
And in a flash he is gone
Just another killing
At this place called The Somme

Battlefield Trees

Twisted and lifeless they stand
Pointing jaggedly in defiance
To the sky

Black, charred and fire ravaged
Their roots still anchor what remains
As distant cannon fire
Carries on the breeze

Once they breathed life
Stood tall and proud
Now a torn splinter
Standing naked in the mud and mire

Forever monuments
To the savagery of war
These battlefield once proud giants
Who breath life no more

Shell Hole

British Soldier
The Somme

I open my eyes
And slowly shake my head
Lying in this shell hole
They must have thought I was dead

There are cuts to my face and hands
Other than that I feel fine
But I guess I have been unconscious
For quite some time

I look at the bodies that lie around me
They all look dead
And I choke back my vomit
At the one with no head

Then I see movement
But he is not one of ours
And like me this German boy
Must have been here for hours

We look at each other
And exchange a smile
But I see from his waist down
He is in a mess, so horrible and vile

I try to help him
But where do you start
When a man lies before you
Blown half apart?

So I take him in my arms
And cradle his head
And talk to him gently
Until his eyes say he is dead

Another young life has ended
Another young life is done
Does it really matter anymore
Who lost and who won?

One Day

They lie there at Mons
They lie there at Verdun
They lie there at Passchendaele
At Cambrai and The Somme

They lie there in the mud
They lie there in the dirt
They lie there screaming
In terror, pain and hurt

Some, they lie there limbless
Some, they lie there with no head
Some, they lie there disembowelled
For they are the lifeless and the dead

But one day they will lie together
One day they will all be as one
One day when this war is finally over
And all this killing is done and gone

Burning Flame

Belgium War Widow

A burning flame in my heart
Has now gone
But the love from its heat
Will forever live on

For you were the light in my life
And I thank each day, dear husband
You chose me
As your wife

Happy memories we once knew
When troubles were so far and few
And even when put to the test
Our love was never second best

So I lay this rose on your grave
And think of the sacrifice you and the others gave
So our nation could remain free
But, oh I wish you, my love
Were still here with me

Footprints In The Snow

Russian Infantry
Eastern Front

Where our spirits are going to
I don't really know
But the final sign of our mortal lives
Are our footprints in the snow

For across this winter's battlefield
Red blood now stains the ground
Some of us will be buried here
Some of us never found

For it's all the same on both sides
Be it enemy, friend or foe
Our lives are now finished and melted away
Like our footprints in the snow

Dedicated to the 9 million Russians who lost their lives

Two Brothers

They said
One brother was given a medal
The other was shot at dawn
One brother was a hero
The other wished he'd never been born

They said
One brother was first to volunteer
The other was given a 'feather'
One brother was first out of the trench
The other said, "No, not ever"

They said
One brother died that day
On the German wire
The other received his court marshal
And branded a coward and a liar

They said
One brother was buried with honour
The other buried in shame
But it doesn't really matter anymore
Because they are now both dead, the same

Casualty Of War

British Soldier

I sit all alone
In this room so dark
As happy voices echo
From across the park

People on way
To meet their love
To drink and dance
At the local club

I used to do the same
But not anymore
Now I sit in this wheelchair
Near the bedroom door

All I want
Is to just walk free
But I have nothing left now
Below my knee

My left hand's gone
The right a twisted stump
My muscles they ache
And my body thumps

My mind it plays
Pictures of war
In all its colour
And all its gore

Will someone please take
This pain from my head
For this useless half a man
Would be better off dead

White Crosses

Present Day
France & Belgium

Row on Row
The white crosses glow
In the last of
Autumn's evening sunshine

Each one is inscribed
With the names who have died
A generation
So needlessly wasted

May their names liveth on
From Verdun to the Somme
And may God's peace be
Always with the fallen

My English Rose

A Soldier's Poem

My lovely English Rose
Carries herself with style
She brightens my life
With each and every smile

A heart of gold
With a spirit so true
A tenderness of touch
Oh, how much I love you

Selfless to the end
My one true friend
An angel from heaven
On whom I can always depend

So with every breath of this life
Be forever my wife
My one and only
True love

Polygon Wood

(Ghost Soldiers)
1917

I wake up in the mud
It seems from a sleep of a thousand years
And look all around me
At the angel's crying tears

For in this earth's filth
Lies a dozen men
Each body drenched in blood
And flashing explosions
Of artillery shells
And constant cannon thud

Then I suddenly realise
As an angel takes my hand
That I am now looking down
At myself lying dead on the ground

For I am no longer living
No longer flesh and blood
As I join the ghost soldiers
And march out of Polygon Wood

Suicide

They pinned a medal on my chest
For extreme bravery under fire
But now I walk a tightrope
Now I walk the wire

'A medal for a hero' the newspapers said
'This man who shows no fear'
But inside my heart, I long to scream
And forever shed a tear

For I left something out there
In the misery of Flanders Fields
Now I have a wound that lives inside my head
The type that never heals

And as I put this rope around my neck
And let my body fall to the floor
Please dear love, forgive me
But I just couldn't take no more

Dedicated to the thousands of soldiers from all countries
Who took their own lives following the end of the Great War

Albert Ball

He flew from Marieux
By dawn's early light
The trenches of the front line
Coming into sight

Moving high into position
And looking down below
There was the enemy
Flying row on row

Now in attack formation
And coming in from the sun
The aerial death show
Has just begun

Into the enemy
From all sides
This is a dogfight
There's nowhere to hide

And in this game
Played out in the sky
The rules are simple
But the stakes are high

For he is the English
Ace of them all
Nottingham's finest
Albert Ball

Dedicated to Capt. Albert Ball
1896-1917

Capt. Ball was officially credited with 44 combat victories and was highly decorated, receiving The Military Cross, The Distinguished Service Order, The Russian order of St George and the French Chevalier De Legion D'Honneur, as well as The Victoria Cross, Posthumously.

He was killed in May 1917. A sad end to a brave and fearless fighter ace.

Vimy Ridge

Canadian Corps
1917

They came to take the high ground
And that's just what they did
And they were that day immortalised
For the capture of Vimy Ridge

The French had bravely tried before them
To take this strategic ground
But each time they were beaten back
No way it seemed could be found

With tremendous courage and bravery
They stepped into life's proud history
Sweeping through the German lines
And achieving their victory

So at the 11th hour we will salute them
The heroes of that day
A great sacrifice for liberty
Soured by the cost in lives to pay

Dedicated to the Canadian Infantry who took this vital strategic ridge line on 9th April 1917 with the award of 4 Victoria Crosses for extreme bravery under fire

Hold The Line

German Infantry Passchendaele

Flakes of snow
Blow across the battlefield
Winter's icy chill it fills the air
The men dug deep in our trenches
Check their rifles and quietly we prepare

'No man's land' lies before us
Cold, frozen and austere
With dry mouthed anticipation we wait
Our stomachs full of fear

"Hold the line at all costs" says Herr Leutnant
The order has been passed down
"We have to do it
A way just has to be found"

"Here they come" came the cry
As the Tommies climb up from their trenches
And hundreds of them are soon through
And over our barbed wire fences
Now they are among us
And we are soon fighting hand to hand
With bayonets and shovels
On this blood spattered land

The screams of pain, terror and death
They soon fill the air
As like crazed beasts we hack at each other
To live, our only care

But somehow we hold them off
And the moment is soon ours
Another day of bloodshed
Among winter's cold, snow showers

Dedicated to the 7 million German casualties

Endless Scream

I walk the battlefield again
Most every night
And I see the enemy
I used to fight

Screaming in torment
In a black hell fire
I see them writhing
In fields of barbed wire

Shells explode
The air's full of gas and smoke
Their lungs burst
As they gasp and choke

With bulging eyes
They twist and turn
Their bodies on fire
As they start to burn

Mouths wide open
In an endless scream
They stumble and fall
In this nightmare scene

A crescendo of noise
And machine gun fire
Bullets spark off
The rusting wire

A river now runs
Full of rain and mud
Mixed with the crimson
Colour of men's blood

Like an artillery shell
My head explodes
As the gas engulfs
My mouth and nose

It's then I awake
Lying in my bed
The cannons still firing
Inside my head

They call it 'shell shock'
This living with the damned
As I spend another night
In this 'no man's land'

Welcome To Hell

U.S. Soldier

On my first day
In the front line trenches
An English Officer
Said these words to me

"Life is fragile son
Here at its best
So keep your head down
And do your best"

"On the offensive
Or if under attack
When the whistle blows
There's no going back"

"Be it in the rain and snow
Mud or ice
There's not much point here
In you praying to Christ"

"For its bayonets and gas
Shot and shell
Lice and rats, son
Welcome to Hell"

Mutineers

French Infantry
Verdun

Rumours abound all along the front line
Of soldiers mutineering and refusing to fight
Whole units totally rebelling
And then disappearing off into the night

Our Captain Henri looks worried
And so he should be
For there's many a man here would like to kill him
And one of them is definitely me

For he and his bastard officers
Have their hands soaked in our comrade's blood
For we have seen our friends die for nothing
Now we are going to avenge them and that's understood

For us it doesn't really matter
Whether we die from a bullet be it German or French
For we are already like the walking dead
Rotting away here in this trench

So the time has now come to kill them
Not for the glory of France
But in the name of honour for our comrades
And to give us living a chance

Dedicated to the thousands of French soldiers who refused to be used as 'cannon fodder' anymore by their Generals and Officers at Verdun, and who were executed by firing squad or otherwise for the crime of only wanting to live

Why?

Like macabre decorations
Our dead hang on their wire
The others that are left alive
Have lungs full of fire

The gas has now cleared
But many lie dead on the ground
The wounded shuffle along in line
As the blind lead the blind

For these boys this war is over
And those left will probably die
I ask what the hell is it all for
I ask the reason WHY?

Rain

British Soldier
Passchendaele

All along this wasted land
The rain keeps pouring down
Filling the shell holes and trenches
And soaking through the ground

Up to our knees in water
Cold and wet through to bone and skin
Mud slides a constant problem
As the trench walls forever collapse in

No need to worry about a bullet
For old 'trench foot' will get you first
You might die of a thousand deaths out here
But it will never be of thirst

And just to add to the misery
The German's hit us with shot and shell
So naturally we reply
And give them a dose as well

The politicians, generals and those butchers
Haig, Nivelle and Foch
They sit somewhere in a nice, warm place
While we 'cannon fodder' cop the lot

If I could have my way
I would gladly bayonet them all

Those war-mongering, murdering bastards
Be rid of them once and for all

But we know that will never happen
Because for us it just constantly rains death
So we will carry on with the misery and slaughter
Until I guess there is nothing left

The Chaplin's Ghost

British Soldier

I remember 'The Front' one winter's night
Thinking of family and friends back home
When I suddenly realised
I was no longer standing alone

For there right beside me
How he got there I will never know
Was a Reverend Army Chaplin
Standing, smiling in the snow

He gently spoke words of wisdom
And said everything would be alright
And no matter whatever happened
I would always survive the fight

Has his words took away
All the thoughts that I had feared
I glanced away for a moment
When I looked back, he had disappeared

I looked up and down the trench
To see where he had gone
It's then I noticed no footprints
In the snow he had just stood on

I asked the lads the next morning
If the Reverend they had seen
But they just laughed and said
"You must have seen him in a dream"

Now the guns no longer thunder
And the fighting has now all gone
But I will never forget that meeting
With the ghostly Chaplain on the Somme

Cold Sweat

French Soldier
Mourmelon

He lies there before me
Blood pouring from his side
The bayonet wound I have given him
Is so cruelly deep and wide

I thrust again at his throat
And the blood begins to spurt
He screams a last deathly cry
As he dies here in the dirt

Just a young boy
A young boy like me
Who only speaks a different language
But was my war adversary

Now each night I wake up
In a pool of 'cold sweat'
His young face forever in my dreams
And that day I can never forget

Dying Alone

Australian Soldier Bellicourt

My life blood pours from me
In this place so far from home
Into the soil of a foreign field
Mortally wounded and all alone

As I slowly fade away
Images are clear of times before
Walking together in warm sunshine
As the blue sea caresses the shore

To die and lose one's life
Is something we all must eventually face
But to die in battle this terrible way
Seems such a pity and a waste

But now as I feel death embrace me
My thoughts are of you and Australia, my home
Please, my darling, stay with me
For I am so scared of dying alone

Walking Dead

Have you ever walked in Hell?
Then know my shoes will fit you well
For I have been to a place
Seen war's suffering and all the waste

Now it lives on inside my head
The grotesque bodies of the dying and the dead
Images explode like cannon fire
With incredible noise as the battle rages higher

Day or night
It's all the same
As I balance a tight wire
Between sane and insane

My mind
It feels as heavy as lead
For now I am one
Of the walking dead

Barbed Wire

I am coiled or straight
Twisted and long
I stretch all the way
From Verdun to the Somme

I am sharp as a razor
And I cut to the bone
The killing fields of war
Is where I call home

And if you try to break me
I will always hit back
And I will smother you
When you try to attack

Also, my friends behind me
Will be waiting for you
And the fire from their machine guns
Will tear you in two

For I am your nightmare
In these fields I know well
And you will always find me
In the place you call Hell

Battlefield Ghosts

When the cemetery gates close
And all the living have gone
We dead walk again
The old battlefields of the Somme

We often meet the enemy
Those boys we used to fight
And talk about the old days
Long into the night

For here, there is no hatred
And the pain has long since gone
Now we are peaceful souls
United all as one

But we always ask the question
Why we were chosen to die
But before we find the answer
A new dawn it fills the sky

So we say Goodbye, auf Wiedersehen
And take our place of rest in gardens of stone
For the killing fields of Flanders
Will forever be our home

Brothers In Arms

11th November 1918
British Infantry

The quietness is almost deafening
Across this wasted land
The guns are no longer firing
There's silence, no sound

I look at the men beside me
They all look lost
With thoughts inside their heads
At what this silence cost

For we are the ones who have made it
Through this terrible war
And I know their thoughts are just like mine
Of comrades no more

I think of Pat, a good friend
Killed at 'The Bluff'
And Bill and Frank you could always depend on
When the going got rough
Chris' words of wisdom
Johnny's endless jokes
Who would have bet they all would be
First past the post

Then I think of that young lad
Just sixteen on that day
When the German gas took him down
And choked his life away

Brothers in arms together
Friends and comrades on whom you could depend
Now just a simple cross marks
Their final life's end

Victoria Cross

I am the cross of valour
Given to the finest and the brave
For extreme courage under fire
And the comrade's lives they saved

For in the intense heat of conflict
As the battle it raged higher
They sacrificed their own lives
In wars burning flames of fire

And on the roll call of honour
Their names will forever be etched on me
For I am the cross of valour
The Victoria Cross, V.C.

Where The Fallen Sleep

The old owl hoots
His haunting cry
Across these fields
Where they came to die

And in the graveyard
White headstones stand
Foreign soldiers buried
In a foreign land

In perfect lines
They lay row on row
Hundred of stones
Now covered in snow

And nothing stirs
As the snowflakes fall
The only sound
Is the old owl's call

Night time silence
As the snow drifts deep
In this place where forever
The fallen shall sleep

Coming Home

To Canada
1918

I walk down the ship's gangway
To the cheering crowds on the dock
But the same man that 4 years ago left here
I am afraid I am not

For I have been to that hell
For so long
An inferno of destruction
That nightmare called the Somme

There I have witnessed
The terrible spilling of men's blood
And seen their lifeless bodies
Lying broken in the mud

But now I return to my Canada
This land I love so dear
No more endless misery
No more deathly fear

And there she is waiting
With a smile and arms held open wide
As I push my way through the crowds
To hold her at my side

And so I kiss her lovingly
With tears of joy and pain
And hope I can find the man I used to be
And become myself again

Dedicated to the soldiers of Canada who fought with great courage and distinction, and whose contribution to the allied victory was immense.

A Soldier's Tears

British Soldier
1919

Once I was a young man
But in this war, I have grown old in years
Still, one thing that always touches my heart
Is the sight of a soldier's tears

Strong men baptised in conflict
At the sharp end of war
With hearts that are broken
And filled with hate no more

Standing to attention
We survivors hear the 'Last Post'
And remember our friends and brothers
Now the battlefields new ghosts

For they are with us always
In the earth and in the sky
And we will forever make sure
That their memory will never die

And later on this evening
As we raise a glass to the brave
To honour the sacrifice of each one
For King and Country, their lives they gave

A Soldier Of The Great War

Nothing remains of me
I cannot be found
For I lie somewhere amongst
This battle scared ground

Just another casualty
Of the Great War
Who fought for my Country
But exist no more

They carved out some words
On white marbled stone
My last resting place far from my home

But sometimes I still walk
Out there on the Somme
A ghost of the past
Now 90 years on

For I am the man
They could find no name for
And my stone simply reads
"A Soldier
of
The Great War"

Armistice Day

Out in Flanders Fields
Summer to autumn yields
And leafless trees now sway
Time to remember the fallen
It's Armistice Day

In once these fields that roared with thunder
Lay the remains of many a good man under
This earth torn so hard
Drenched in blood
And long since battle scared

But today on the hour we will remember
These brave souls now all gone
Of their sacrifice and courage
May forever their memory
Always live on

To End All Wars

"The war to end all wars"
That's what they said
Monuments and crosses
Commemorate the missing and the dead

Millions of men
From all corners of the globe
They all died young
So can never grow old

And all across 'the front'
Lie gardens of stone
The last resting place for so many
Far from their home

For you can put out the fire
And extinguish the flame
But let the candle of peace
Always burn in their name

Dedicated to the 37 million casualties of the Great War from all countries.

ND - #0111 - 060826 - C0 - 210/148/6 - PB - 9781780354712 - Gloss Lamination